T5-CVG-063

In the same series:
Love, a celebration (1981)
Marriage, a keepsake (1982)
For Mother, a gift of love (1983)
Love is a Grandmother (1983)

Also edited by Helen Exley:
Grandmas and Grandpas (1975)
To Mum (1976)
To Dad (1976)
Happy Families (1977)
What is a Husband? (1977)
Cats (and other crazy cuddlies) (1978)
Dogs (and other funny furries) (1978)
Dear World (1978)
A Child's View of Happiness (1979)
A Child's View of Christmas (1980)
What is a Baby? (1980)
What it's like to be me (1981)
What is a Wife? (1982)
A Gift of Flowers (1983)

Published by Exley Publications Ltd, 16 Chalk Hill,
Watford, Herts, United Kingdom WD1 4EN
Selection and design © Exley Publications Ltd 1983
First published in Great Britain 1983

Printed in Great Britain by Butler & Tanner Ltd, Frome

British Library Cataloguing in Publication Data
For grandad, a gift of love.
    1. Grandfathers – Literary collections
    I. Exley, Helen
820.8'0352'0432   PR1111.G/

ISBN 0-905521-93-5

FOR GRANDAD
a gift of love

Edited by Helen Exley

EXLEY

ASSORTED GRANDADS

A grandfather is someone who has at last discovered that only people matter.

A grandfather is someone who doesn't care if you've got on the wrong socks. He probably has too.

Grandchildren are going where you'll never go. And you've been where they can never go. So you've got a lot to talk about.

Real grandads are younger than all the story books. But they snore just as loud.

A grandfather is a man whose eyesight, hearing, teeth, legs, stamina, memory and virility aren't what they were – but who seems to be exactly right for being a grandad.

A grandfather is someone who has the same sort of vices as his grandchildren – toffees, peppermints, dawdling, coming in late for meals and leaving his greens.

It's only when you have grandchildren that you realise all the best books in the library are in the children's section.

When the afternoon seems to be disintegrating into a catastrophe of biscuit crumbs and spilled tea, your grandchild leans across the ruin with infinite love and offers you a soggy Garibaldi. 'Womp wum ganda?'

. . .Well, after all, a quick run round with the cleaner when they are gone . . .

Grandads who have weathered decades of reproach and warning from their children on the subject of cigarette smoking, give it up overnight when their grandchildren burst into tears and beg them not to die.

GRANDADS DEFINED

Grandchildren are genuinely interested in
spectacles, false teeth, prescriptions, hair pieces,
pills and wheezes in the chest and knobbly joints
which makes the dire collection rather less
melancholy.

It's not wise to send Grandad up the road with his
grandchild to get the ice-cream. They have to
exchange courtesies with every perching cat, smell
half a dozen roses, look down a hole, watch a
caterpillar progress the length of a twig, talk to two
old ladies and another small child, pick up a stone
for Mummy and stand perfectly still while a
black-bird catches his dinner.
Better make it tinned peaches.

Grandads must get used to being examined with
loving and meticulous care, like a rare mummy.

Parents secretly want their kids to be the success
they weren't. Granpas want their grandchildren to
be happy.

Grandads only get really mad if you hide their
teeth.

No, dear, Napoleon wasn't in Grandad's war.

Grandads lack nothing but puff.

Grandads are dignified men who run after backing cars waving the forgotten potty.

Every child needs to run away from home once in its life. Best place is to Grandad's. Phone first.

Grandads love their grandchildren very much – but never enough to enjoy eating half-eaten titbits from sticky fingers. That's not to say they don't do it.

Matthew Kent, age 8

CONFORM – DON'T TRY TO CHANGE THE RULES

The rituals of grandfatherhood were established generations ago and nothing you can do will change them. Though you be a soldier, tycoon, explorer or intellectual, folklore has it that the grandchild will bedazzle you, rob you of your senses, reduce you to a jellylike blob of emotion. And folklore is correct.

You are *expected* to boast. Why not do so? You are *expected* to see your grandchild as the most beautiful and intelligent baby ever born. Why try to be modest? For the first time in your life you are *expected* to indulge yourself. So don't knock the system.

That's all the time I have for advice – there's a car coming up the drive bringing Jennifer for a visit. She knows me now and always greets me with a smile of incandescent radiance. Her parents and her grandmother claim it is the same smile she gives them, but I know the difference. Jennifer and I know the difference.

Floyd Miller

SO WILL I

My grandfather remembers long ago
the white Queen Anne's lace that grew wild.
He remembers the buttercups and goldenrod
from when he was a child.

He remembers long ago
the white snow falling falling.
He remembers the bluebird and thrush
at twilight
calling, calling.

He remembers long ago
The new moon in the summer sky
He remembers the wind in the trees
and its long, rising sigh.
And so will I
          so will I.

Charlotte Zolotow

PARENTS ARE THE COMMON ENEMY!

What has been called the 'love affair' between the first and third generations has long been known to sociologists who still have never explored this 'in depth' with barrels of statistics. A few years ago, one treatise pointed out a bit timidly that grandparents and grandchildren share a common enemy, the parents, against whom they must constantly plot in conspirators' glee. Grandfathers, grandmothers and grandchildren have never needed to be told this; they instinctively sense they have supporters and defenders in each other. 'Grandma stands out as Public Defender Number One. Nobody in Washington or any world capital can match her,' is Sam's salute. 'Remember how our own mother wanted to tear us from limb to limb at any provocation? Now it's the same woman who says sharply to her daughter, "Don't you touch him. Reason with him. Did I ever hit you?" All the kid was doing was sawing a leg off the dining room table. Says Grandma: "He's just playing." '

Helen Alpert, in an article about Sam Levenson

A FLOWER FOR GRANDAD

To meet this small creature,
her whole self
intent on this one purpose, the offering of a flower,
is to be other than I am.
Her eyes are full of the search for words,
the story of its finding
– but only
'Grandad! Flower!'

bridges the space between us.
I scoop her up.
We smile, delighted by each other's presence.
This warm complexity
that owes its being to my own;
this child
to whom I am more special
than man has any right to be.

Peter Gray

I'm fifty now and tired and fat and out of breath –
but I can still feel my hand – a skinny, bony hand,
not this blotched paw – in his. Engulfed. Safe and
sound in that great, brown hand that smelled of
Lifebuoy and shag. Part of me still walks those
drowsy lanes – long overcome by concrete – with
him, under those distant skies of summer.

P. Brown

WHAT IS A GRANDFATHER?

He's an 'authority', they say, and it's true. He really can fix a skate and build a kennel and fly a kite.

He understands you when you cry and he understands people except he says he doesn't ever pretend to understand a woman. That's when his eyes twinkle most.

His legs are getting kind of bony but he still lets you sit on his lap even when your legs are almost as long as his.

He knows all kinds of fascinating stories and he must have lived a lot of places and met a lot of people and done a lot of things. He's just about the most interesting person I expect I'll ever meet but in his stories he always makes the other people the interesting ones.

I don't think Grandpa was ever a little boy – yet he says he was. He acts like it sometimes with other grown-ups when he doesn't think there are any little kids around. Maybe that's why grown-ups like him so much.

Harry McMahan

COME ON IN, THE SENILITY IS FINE

People live forever in Jacksonville and St.
    Petersburg and Tampa,
But you don't have to live forever to become a
    grampa.
The entrance requirements for grampahood are
    comparatively mild,
You only have to live until your child has a child.
From that point on you start looking both ways
    over your shoulder,
Because sometimes you feel thirty years younger
    and sometimes thirty years older.

Now you begin to realize who it was that reached
the height of imbecility,
It was whoever said that grandparents have all the
fun and none of the responsibility.
This is the most enticing spiderweb of a tarradiddle
ever spun,
Because everybody would love to have a baby
around who was no responsibility and lots of
fun,
But I can think of no one but a mooncalf or a gaby
Who would trust their own child to raise a baby.
So you have to personally superintend your
grandchild from diapers to pants and from
bottle to spoon
Because you know that your own child hasn't sense
enough to come in out of a typhoon.
You don't have to live forever to become a grampa,
but if you do want to live forever,
Don't try to be clever;
If you wish to reach the end of the trail with an
uncut throat,
Don't go around saying Quote I don't mind being a
grampa but I hate being married to a gramma
Unquote.

Ogden Nash

PREFACE TO THE PAST

Time all of a sudden tightens the tether,
And the outspread years are drawn together.
How confusing the beams from memory's
    lamp are;
One day a bachelor, the next a grampa.
What is the secret of the trick?
How did I get so old so quick?
Perhaps I can find by consulting the files
How step after step added up to miles.
I was sauntering along, my business minding,
When suddenly struck by affection blinding,
Which led to my being a parent nervous
Before they invented the diaper service.
I found myself in a novel pose,

Counting infant fingers and toes.
I tried to be as wise as Diogenes
In the rearing of my two little progenies,
But just as I hit upon wisdom's essence

They changed from infants to adolescents.
I stood my ground, being fairly sure
That one of these days they must mature,
So when I was properly humbled and harried,
They did mature, and immediately married.
Now I'm counting, the cycle being complete,
The toes on my children's children's feet.
Here lies my past, good-by I have kissed it;
Thank you, kids, I wouldn't have missed it.

Ogden Nash

All that I ever was is in this skin,
selves folded wafer thin
and packed about the bone.
I live a multitude of men
and yet alone.
My grandchild, no philosopher at three,
ignoring this complexity,
demands a story of the current me.

Peter Gray

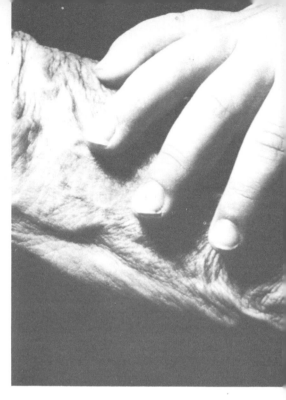

JUST TALKING

One of the most original men I know used to be left
as a very small child to care for his immobilized but
alert grandfather, and they spent long hours talking
together. Today, at sixty-five, he is one of the most
inspired *futurists* I know. He learned how to think

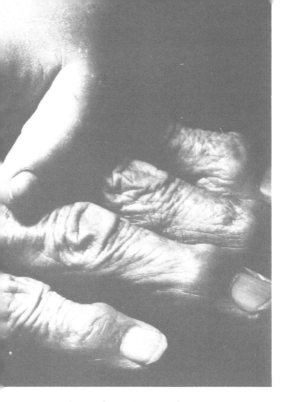

about the future from his grandfather, who, sitting helpless in a wheelchair, had time for endless speculative, entrancing conversations. And today young people swarm around him wherever he goes. So the felicity of a contact that occurred sixty-three years ago is carried on and recreated today.

Margaret Mead

TIME TO FLY

Straight from the grandparent front, a story. I've heard it in several versions, but this one I need for my grandfathering.

Ronnie was twelve. Outside his bedroom window he spotted a grey cocoon. Grandpa told him if he watched it closely, that ball of fuzz would break open and out would come a butterfly.

Sure enough, that's exactly what happened. Only it took so long. Before he knew it, Ronnie was pushing and straining too. Suddenly, he had a bright idea. He would take his knife and cut around the end to set the butterfly free. Beautiful!

Only, you know! Sad! Several times the butterfly tried to take off, but couldn't. So at last it gave up and died. What would you do if you were a little boy with a dead butterfly in your hand and wonder in your eyes? Well, if you had a grandpa in the house like this little boy's grandpa, you'd go to him. And you would learn something important when he said, 'Ronnie, the butterfly needed to fight its way out. That's how it gets strength to fly.'

Fine lesson for a child, isn't it? And should I be doing a retake on the same lesson for my grandchildren? In any case, am I cutting the cocoon too soon?

Charlie W. Shedd

MADE IN HEAVEN

We ignore grandfathers at our peril – one of them is looking over my shoulder as I write. They strengthen and sustain us, they keep us from committing grandmotherly follies, and they make their own contribution to the grandchildren's lives. But everyone seems to agree with me that grandfathers need no book to reassure, encourage or advise them. Grandfathers are made in heaven, born fully formed with the birth of their first grandchild. They are the perfect babysitters, storytellers, playmates, and putters-to-bed. Their role is pure delight.

Ruth Goode, from 'A Book for Grandmothers'

IN A CHANGING WORLD

Grandparents need grandchildren to keep the
changing world alive for them. And grandchildren
need grandparents to help them know who they are
and to give them a sense of human experience in a
world they cannot know. In the past this was
literally so. Now and in the future, when more
adults will be concerned with the care of young
children who are not their own descendants, this
remains a model of mutual learning across
generations.

Margaret Mead

To every child since the world began that first lurching step has been a triumph; to each its first confrontation with thunder, snow, fire, a star-packed heaven, a silent forest, a mountain rearing from the plain, the sea itself, has been a miracle. Small things, too. The wicked delights of chocolate revealed in a bag of Buttons; the cold, sweet, uncontrollable marvel of the first ice-cream cone; the first ride on a merry-go-round, clutched to grandad's chest; the unimaginable excitement of the bumps and lumps of the first Christmas stocking.

The Teens bring the terrors, far worse than that first ill-tempered dog, that first clattering, strange-smelling visit to a hospital. The first warm, shapeless, disappointing kiss; the first real party, where not a single face seems familiar; the first really vital examination and the fateful envelope that follows in its wake.

First pay packet and its attendant euphoria and over-spending. First car; every rust patch, every flake of chrome, every near-matching touching up known as intimately as his own body.

And other glories. First flight, the sea like lace along the edges of the land, the first sounds and smells of a country not his own. Faces. Hands. The incredible discovery of love. First home. First child.

And now he discovers all his firsts again, through these new eyes, and things he had never noticed before this child discovered them for him.

Time runs, grows repetitious. The firsts are fewer now – perhaps he has no chance to look about him, perhaps he fails to make those chances.

And now he is middle-aged, and even magic has grown a little stale. Roses are roses. One spring is very like another.

Until one day someone puts a small, shawl-wrapped creature in his arms – his first grandchild. And suddenly the world is full of possibilities again, of shining firsts for him to share and savour.

P. Brown

CONSOLATION FOR BALDNESS

What's the advantage of hair, anyhow?
It blows in your eyes and it flops on your brow,
Disguising the shape of your scholarly head;
It often is grey and it sometimes is red.
Perhaps it is golden and ringleted, but
It needs to be combed and it has to be cut,
And even at best it is nothing to boast of
Because it's what barbarous men have the most of;
Then challenge your mirror, defiant and careless,
For lots of our handsomest people are hairless.

Arthur Guiterman

from ME AND GRANDAD'S MATES . . .

Grandad takes me fishin' on a Saturday
Me 'n' Grandad's mates
Grandad brings me maggots pink 'n' yeller uns
And me hooks and weights
We fish all day come rain or shine
On the banks of the old canal
Sometimes we say nowt
Other days we chat away
'Cos me 'n' Grandad's pals.

Grandad takes me walkin' with his little dog
He calls her Gyp
We go to the pub and Grandad has a pint of Grog
Gives me a sip
He says he drinks beer 'cos his legs are stiff
An' it oils them 'n' makes 'em supple
Sometimes I think it works too well
'Cos it doesn't half make him wobble.

Grandad he comes round and sits with me
When Mam and Dad go out
We play snakes and ladders and Monopoly
Grandad has a bottle of stout
He lets me stay up till half-past ten
And if Mam asks him what time
He made me go upstairs to bed
Grandad says half-past nine.

Grandad shows me tricks with pennies
Grandad flies me kite
Grandad brings me fish 'n' chips
Home from the pub at night
And if ever I grow up and I get old
And my kids have kids
Then I'll take 'em fishin' and do all the other things
That me Grandad did.

Mike Harding

RAILINGS

towards the end of his tether
grandad
at the drop of a hat
would paint the railings

overnight
we became famous
allover the neighbourhood
for our smart railings

(and our dirty hats)

Roger McGough

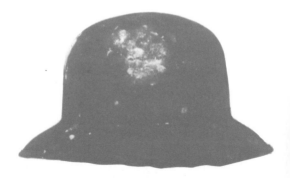

BUCKET

everyevening after tea
grandad would take his bucket for a walk

An empty bucket

When i asked him why
he said because it was easier to carry

grandad had
an answer
for everything

Roger McGough

MY WISE OLD GRANDPAPA

When I was but a little chap
My grandpapa said to me,
'You'll need to know your manners, son
When you go out to tea.

'Remove the shells from hard-boiled eggs,
Make sure your hat's on straight,
Pour lots of honey on your peas
To keep them on the plate.

'Blow daintily upon your tea
To cool it to your taste,
And always pick bones thoroughly,
With due regard for waste.

'Be heedful of your partners' needs,
Attend their every wish;
When passing jelly, cream or jam,
Make sure they're in the dish.

'When eating figs or coconuts,
To show you are refined,
Genteelly gnaw the centres out
And throw away the rind.

'If you should accidentally gulp
Some coffee while it's hot,
Just raise the lid politely and
Replace it in the pot.

'Don't butter ice cream when it's warm,
Or drink soup through a straw.'
Thus spoke my wise old grandpapa
When I was only four.

Wilbur G. Howcroft

GRANDFATHER

They brought him in on a stretcher from the world,
Wounded but humorous. And he soon recovered.
Boiler-rooms, row upon row of gantries rolled
Away to reveal the landscape of a childhood
Only he can recapture. Even on cold
Mornings he is up at six with a block of wood
Or a box of nails, discreetly up to no good
Or banging round the house like a four-year-old –

Never there when you call. But after dark
You hear his great boots thumping in the hall
And in he comes, as cute as they come. Each night
His shrewd eyes bolt the door and set the clock
Against the future, then his light goes out.
Nothing escapes him; he escapes us all.

Derek Mahon

FAIR EXCHANGE

My grandfather stood tree tall;
cared not at all for midget men in Cadillacs
but gave them time of day
and went his way, striding toward the sun.
Or so it seemed to me,
scuttling at his knee, and bound for glory.
Time brought him down,
carted him off to town and set him in a chair
to rock away the hours.
Ma took him flowers. But me, I took him tales
of far away, and he,
he ran along with me, living the story.

P. Brown

OLD MAN PLAYING WITH CHILDREN

A discreet householder exclaims on the grandsire
In warpaint and feathers, with fierce grandsons and
    axes
Dancing round a backyard fire of boxes:
'Watch grandfather, he'll set the house on fire.'

But I will unriddle for you the thought of his mind,
An old one you cannot open with conversation.
What animates the thin legs in risky motion?
Mixes the snow on the head with snow on the wind?

'Grandson, grandsire. We are equally boy and boy.
Do not offer your reclining-chair and slippers
With tedious old women talking in wrappers.
This life is not good but in danger and in joy.

'It is you the elder to these and younger to me
Who are penned as slaves by properties and causes
And never walk from your shaped insupportable
    houses
And shamefully, when boys shout, go in and flee.

'May God forgive, me, I know your middling ways,
Having taken care and performed ignominies
    unreckoned
Between the first brief childhood and the brief
    second,
But I will be the more honourable in these days.'

John Crowe Ransom

PASSING SOMETHING ON

Janos Koscka is a retired cabinetmaker who learned his craft as a youth in his native Hungary. Peter, his nine-year-old grandson, is learning woodburning from him on the lathe in the basement of the Koscka's two-family house.

In San Francisco's Chinatown, ten-year-old Kim Soong stacks rice cakes, while his sister Lin, eight, wraps them in plastic for the customers in their grandfather's teashop-bakery.

Tom Mundy is spending his sixtieth birthday with his seven-year-old grandson Dennis. They are sitting in comfortable silence in a rowing boat in the middle of a lake, waiting patiently for the fish to bite.

These three grandfathers are sharing something precious – and unfortunately rare these days – with their grandchildren, to the benefit of both generations. Passing on skills, transmitting family history, giving the young their first chance to be of real help, or just being there in undemanding companionship – these are some of the roles grandparents have played since history began. Doing so has given a fuller meaning, an extra dimension to the lives of young people and older ones, too. In fact, it is what makes a family a family.

Rita Kramer

TOMORROW'S WORLD

Many of today's young appear to be completely turned off by any idea from yesterday. Some of them really are. Forever.

But countless of these who appear to be turned off aren't really that turned off. They aren't that turned off to democracy. They aren't that turned off to our constitutional heritage. Nor to history. What they are turned off to is any of us who are overly turned on to days gone by.

As I rap with them, I find they are willing to see good in the past, provided. Provided what? Provided I remain flexible enough to believe:

(a) All the good hasn't been done.

(b) They can make a contribution too.

So here is another absolute essential if I am to communicate with my grandchildren. I must have in my head and heart a touch of the poet's philosophy:

> The best verse hasn't been rhymed yet.
> The best world hasn't been planned.

Charlie W. Shedd

Life is no brief candle to me. It is a sort of splendid torch which I have got hold of for the moment, and I want to make it burn as brightly as possible before handing it on to future generations.

George Bernard Shaw

BREATHING PURELY

Now, at last,
I carry nothing
In my briefcase
And an empty mind.
In the meadow

Under the chestnut tree
I am a part of what I see.
Swallows above the alder thicket
Skim mosquitoes from the haze,
And I've seceded

From all committees, left
My Letters to the Editor unsent
No solutions, no opinions.
Breathing purely
Without ambitions, purged, awaiting

Annunciations of the true.
The wind is up now and the swallows gone.
I'll listen to the chestnut tree
Rustling
Empty-headed in the wind.

Daniel Hoffman

Leave the flurry
To the masses;
Take your time
And shine your glasses.

Old Shaker Verse

TO MY GRANDCHILDREN

You are too young as yet,
My dears,
For me to tell you what I owe.
And so,
Against the day
When you are tall
And I am clay,
I must record my debt.
If in the coming years
Your eyes chance on these pages,
You will not find that Grandad was
Among the prophets or the sages.
But should you catch, within this looking-glass,
Some hint at all
Of worthy vision, thought or aim:
Well, then, I guess
It mostly came
From love of such as you. God bless!

Gilbert Thomas

GRANDAD

Heaven's mighty sweet, I guess;
Ain't no rush to git there;
Been a sinner, more or less;
Maybe wouldn't fit there.
Wicked still, bound to confess;
Might jest pine a bit there.

Heaven's swell, the preachers say:
Got so used to earth here;
Had such good times all the way,
Frolic, fun and mirth here;
Eighty Springs ago today,
Since I had my birth here.

Quite a spell of happy years.
Wish I could begin it;
Cloud and sunshine, laughter, tears,
Livin' every minute.
Women, too, the pretty dears;
Plenty of 'em in it.

Heaven! that's another tale.
Mightn't let me chew there.
Gotta have me pot of ale;
Would I like the brew there?
Maybe I'd get slack and stale –
No more chores to do there.

Here I weed the garden plot,
Scare the crows from pillage;
Simmer in the sun a lot,
Talk about the tillage.
Yarn of battles I have fought,
Greybeard of the village.

Heaven's mighty fine, I know . . .
Still, it ain't so bad here.
See them maples all aglow;
Starlings seem so glad here:
I'll be mighty peeved to go,
Scrumptious times I've had here.

Lord, I know You'll understand.
With Your Light You'll lead me.
Though I'm not the pious brand,
I'm here when You need me.
Gosh! I know that Heaven's GRAND,
But dang it! God, *don't speed me.*

Robert Service

I had my second childhood rather early – about two years after my first grandchild was born. I enjoyed mud pies and squodgy jelly and squeaky teddies more than he did! I've been through that stage at least ten times now and when the joy dies I know I will be old.

Oliver Sugden

THE GATHERING

At my age my father
held me on his arm
like a hooded bird,
and his father held him so.
Now I grow into brotherhood
with my father as he
with his has grown,
time teaching me
his thoughts in my own.
Now he speaks in me
as when I knew him first,
as his father spoke
in him when he had come
to thirst for the life
of a young son. My son
will know me in himself
when his son sits hooded on
his arm and I have grown
to be brother to all
my fathers, memory
speaking to knowledge,
finally, in my bones.

Wendell Berry

GRANDFATHER

I remember
His sparse white hair and lean face . . .
Creased eyes that twinkled when he laughed
And the sea-worn skin
Patterned to a latticework of lines.
I remember
His blue-veined, calloused hands,
Long gnarled fingers
Stretching out towards the fire –
Three fingers missing –
Yet he was able to make model yachts
And weave baskets.
Each bronzed Autumn
He would gather berries.
Each breathing Spring
His hands were filled with flowers.
I remember
Worshipping his fisherman's yarns,
Watching his absorbed expression
As he solved the daily crossword
With the slim cigarette, hand rolled,
Placed between his lips.
I remember
The snowdrops,
The impersonal hospital bed,
The reek of antiseptic.

I remember, too,
The weeping child
And wilting daffodils
Laid upon his grave.

Susan Hrynkow, aged 13

MOORS (FOR MY GRANDFATHER)

Born where the moors end,
crag rock and pitted landscape,
you enter again my dreams,
strange visitor in a cold room.

Once again, I remember your stories:
'Faith Smith' and 'Rock' and 'Iron',
the legendary horses of the stream,
the men of the ruined valleys.

In your voice,
a lost world is remembered:
a childhood of hills and stone,
an eternity of chapel and water.

And dark as the soil,
dark as the fathomless centre,
you stand once more in my room,
your eyes staring into silence.

William Bedford

ADVENTURES WITH MY GRANDFATHER

'Once around is enough,' my grandfather said,
plucking me off the merry-go-round.
'We will walk in the park together.'
My hand rested in his big one
as I skipped secret steps to equal his stride.
Pipe fragrance lingered long on my mittens.

Years later, we went to watch Westerns,
balcony-exclusive, in nearby movie houses.
At the end, he was always ready.
Parting with pipe, he cleared his throat:
'You will never enjoy it again like the first time.
Once around is enough.'
I was still learning to leave when a show was over.

A final day: he beyond Westerns and winter walks,
content at his corner window as on a balcony;
surveying far boundaries of park;
reviewing a merry-go-round parade of people below.
As I wondered out loud:
'Would you like to do it all over again, grandpa?'
he managed the longest smile without removing
his pipe – and I knew the answer.

Anne Marx

IN MEMORY OF MY GRANDFATHER

Swearing about the weather he walked in
like an old tree and sat down;
his beard charred with tobacco, his voice
rough as the bark of his cracked hands.

Whenever he came it was the wrong time.
Roots spread over the hearth, tripped
whoever tried to move about the room –
the house was cramped with only furniture.

But I was glad of his coming. Only
through him could I breathe in the sun
and the smell of fields. His clothes reeked
of the soil and the world outside;

Geese and cows were the colour he made them,
he knew the language of birds and brought them
singing out of his beard, alive
to my blankets. He was winter and harvest.

Plums shone in his eyes when he rambled
of orchards. With giant thumbs he'd split
an apple through the core, and juice
flowed from his ripe, uncultured mouth.

Then, hearing the room clock chime,
he walked from my ceiling of farmyards
and returned to his forest of thunder.
The house regained silence and corners.

Slumped there in my summerless season
I longed for his rough hands and words
to break the restrictions of my bed,
to burst like a tree from my four walls.

But there was no chance again of miming
his habits or language. Only now,
years later in a cramped city, can I
be grateful for his influence and love.

Edward Storey

TO GEORGIA, WITH LOVE

While Sam Levenson was finishing *In One Era &
Out the Other*, his granddaughter Georgia was born.
The book's final page is the letter he wrote to her.
'Georgia baby: We leave you a tradition with a
future. The tender loving care of human beings will
never become obsolete. People, even more than
things, have to be restored, renewed, revived,
reclaimed, and redeemed, and redeemed. . . .
Never throw out anybody.

'As you grow older you will discover that you
have two hands. One for helping yourself, the other
for helping others. While I was growing up I took as
many hands as I gave. I still do.

'At our age we doubt whether we will make it to
your wedding, but if you remember us on that day,
we shall surely be there. Mazeltov. . . .' He did not
have to sign it: 'Your Loving Grandfather and
Thank You'.

Helen Alpert

ACKNOWLEDGEMENTS: The publishers gratefully acknowledge permission to reproduce copyright material. Every effort has been made to trace copyright holders, but in a few cases this has proved impossible. The publishers would be interested to hear from any copyright holders not here acknowledged.

HELEN ALPERT, extracts from 'Meet the New Sam Levenson – Grandfather' from the May 1975 issue of *Retirement Living*. Copyright © 1975 by Harvest Years Publishing Co.; ALASDAIR ASTON, *A Striking Old Man*. Reprinted by permission of the author; WILLIAM BEDFORD, 'Moors'. Reprinted by permission of the author; WENDELL BERRY, 'The Gathering', from *The Country of Marriage*, Jovanovich Inc. © 1971/2/3; RUTH GOODE, excerpt from *A Book for Grandmothers*. Reprinted by permission of Macmillan Publishing Company. Copyright © 1976 Ruth Goode; ARTHUR GUITERMAN, 'Consolation for Baldness', from *My Den*; MIKE HARDING, 'Me and Grandad's Mates', reprinted by permission of Moonraker Productions; DANIEL HOFFMAN, 'Breathing Purely' from *Striking the Stones*. (New York & London: Oxford University Press), copyright © 1968 by Daniel Hoffman. Used by permission; WILBUR G. HOWCROFT, 'My Wise Old Grandpapa' from *Stuff and Nonsense* published by Collins; SUSAN HRYNKOW, 'Grandfather' from *Delights & Warnings* published by MacDonald Education. Reprinted by permission of Northwest Arts; RITA KRAMER, excerpt from *Is There a Grandpa in the House?* from the May 1974 issue of *Parents*. Copyright © 1974 Parents Magazine Enterprises. ROGER McGOUGH, 'Bucket' and 'Railings' from *After the Merrymaking*. Reprinted by permission of Jonathan Cape Ltd; HARRY McMAHAN, 'What is a Grandfather?' from *Grandpa was Quite a Boy* by Harry and Gloria McMahan, Escondido, California; DEREK MAHON, 'Grandfather' from *Poems 1962-1978*. Copyright © Derek Mahon 1979. Reprinted by permission of Oxford University Press; ANNE MARX, 'Adventures with my Grandfather' from *The Illustrated Treasury of Poetry for Children* published by Collins (and Grosset and Dunlap). Reprinted by permission of the poet and the publishers; MARGARET MEAD, excerpt from 'Grandparents as Educators' from the December 1974 issue of *Teachers College Record*. Excerpt from 'On being a Grandmother' from *Aspects of the Present* by Margaret Mead and Rhoda Metraux, copyright © 1980 by Mary Katherine Bateson Kassarjian and Rhoda Metraux. Used by permission of the publisher William Morrow & Co, Inc.; FLOYD MILLER, excerpts from *The Expectant Grandfather's Guidebook by Floyd Miller* © 1968 by Harvest Years Publishing Co.; OGDEN NASH, 'Come on In, The Senility is Fine' copyright © 1954 by Ogden Nash, first appeared in *The New Yorker*. 'Preface to the Past' copyright © 1956 by Ogden Nash, first appeared in *Coronet*. Reprinted by permission of Little, Brown and Company and by André Deutsch from the book *I wouldn't have missed it*. 'The Ring in Grandfather's Nose' copyright © 1956 by Ogden Nash, first appeared in *Good Housekeeping*. Reprinted by permission of Little, Brown and Company and Curtis Brown Ltd, London on behalf of the Estate of Ogden Nash; JOHN CROWE RANSOM, 'Old Man Playing with Children' from *Selected Poems* published by Methuen Ltd. Reprinted by permission of Alfred A. Knopf/Random House Inc.; ROBERT SERVICE, 'Grandad' from *The Best of Robert Service* published by Ernest Benn. Reprinted by permission of Heinman & Karsilavsky; GEORGE BERNARD SHAW, excerpt reprinted by permission of The Society of Authors on behalf of the Bernard Shaw Estate; CHARLES W. SHEDD, excerpts from *Then God Created Grandparents*

PHOTOGRAPHS AND ILLUSTRATIONS:

L. C. ALLINGTON: illustrating 'A man's life is full...'; BBC HULTON PICTURE LIBRARY: illustrating 'I'm fifty now...'; JEANNIE BAKER: illustrating 'What is a Grandfather?' From *Grandfather*, published by André Deutsch; JIM BENNETT: illustrating 'Grandfather' by Derek Mahon; RON BROOKS: illustrating 'Fair Exchange', from *Timothy and Gramps* copyright © Ron Brooks 1978, published by Collins; TONY BOXALL/BARNABY'S PICTURE LIBRARY: illustrating 'Leave the flurry...' and 'The Gathering'; DOREEN DAVIES BURROUGHS/BARNABY'S PICTURE LIBRARY: illustrating 'I had my second childhood...'; SUE CURRANT: illustrating 'Passing on Something.'; JOHN EDWARDS: illustrating 'Old Man Playing with Children'; HELEN EXLEY: illustrating 'Breathing Purely'; RICHARD EXLEY: illustrating poems by Roger McGough, 'In a Changing World' 'Advice to Grandfathers' and 'Conform – Don't try to Change the Rules'; IVAN AND JEAN HARRIMAN: illustrating 'Moors' and 'To my Grandchildren'; MAX HUNN/BARNABY'S PICTURE LIBRARY: illustrating 'In Memory of My Grandfather'; SYLVESTER JACOBS: illustrating 'Tomorrow's World'; JEROBOAM INC: illustrating 'To Georgia, with love'. Photograph by Ken Graves; CAMILLA JESSEL: illustrating 'Made in Heaven' and 'Consolation for Baldness'; JOHN TOPHAM PICTURE LIBRARY: illustrating 'Me and Grandad's Mates'; TOM KENNEDY/SOURCE PHOTOGRAPHIC ARCHIVES: illustrating 'Life is no brief candle...' and 'So Will I'; MATTHEW KENT: illustrating 'Grandads Defined'; KEYSTONE PRESS AGENCY LTD: illustrating 'All that I ever was...', photograph by John Arms; LONDON EXPRESS NEWS AND FEATURE SERVICES: illustrating 'My Wise Old Grandpapa'; URSULA LANDSHOFF: illustrating 'Adventures with my Grandfather'. Reprinted by permission of Grosset & Dunlap Inc. from *Illustrated Treasury of Poetry for Children*, © 1976 by Grosset & Dunlap Inc.; MARY EVANS PICTURE LIBRARY: illustrating 'Grandfather' by Susan Hrynkow; MICHAEL MOULDS: illustrating 'A Striking Old Man'; INGER AND LASSE SANDBERG: illustrating 'What has been called the 'love affair'...' Reprinted by permission of Methuen Children's Books, from *Little Anna and the Tall Uncle;* MAURICE SENDAK: illustrating poems by Ogden Nash from *You Can't Get There From Here* by Ogden Nash, drawings by Maurice Sendak. Copyright © 1957 by Ogden Nash. Reprinted by permission of Little Brown and Co.; ANTHEA SIEVEKING: illustrating 'A Flower for Grandad'. Reprinted by permission of Vision International; SYNDICATION INTERNATIONAL: illustrating 'Assorted Grandads'; ROBERT E. TONSING: illustrating 'Grandad' by Robert Service. Reprinted by permission of Colorado Springs Sun; ZEFA PICTURE LIBRARY: illustrating 'Just Talking'.

Other gift books produced by Exley Publications

Love is a Grandmother, £4.95. A companion collection to this volume, bound in soft beige suedel. Writers include Walter de la Mare, Bertrand Russell, Pam Brown, Leonard Clark, Marje Proops and Hilaire Belloc. Giftwrapped with sealing wax.

Love, a Celebration, £4.95. In the same series as this but with a burgundy suedel cover. Writers and poets old and new have captured the feeling of being in love, in this very personal collection. Giftwrapped with sealing wax. Give it to someone special.

Marriage, a Keepsake, £4.95. Also in the same series, but with a dove-grey suedel cover. This collection of poems and prose celebrates marriage with some of the finest love messages between husbands and wives. A gift for all ages – from those about to be married to those who have known fifty good years and more together. Giftwrapped with sealing wax.

For Mother, a gift of love, £4.95. This collection of tributes to mothers is bound in pale blue suedel. Rudyard Kipling, Noël Coward, T. B. Macaulay, Victor Hugo, Norman Mailer, C. Day Lewis and Alfred Lord Tennyson are among the contributors. Giftwrapped with sealing wax.

Grandmas & Grandpas, £3.95. Children are close to grandparents, and this book reflects that warmth. 'A Grandma is old on the outside and young on the inside.' An endearing book for grandparents.

To Dad, £3.95. 'Fathers are always right, and even if they're not right, they're never actually wrong.' Dads will love this book – it's so true to life! A regular favourite.

What is a Baby?, £3.95. Parents and grandparents describe the fun and traumas of bringing up baby. A hilarious and beautiful book for any young mother, stunningly illustrated with beautiful photographs.

What is a Husband?, £3.95. 7,500 real wives attempted to answer the question, and the best quotes are here. Pithy, beautiful, hilarious, sad, romantic – all you might expect. Buy a copy for your anniversary!

Simply order through your bookshop, or by post from Exley Publications Ltd., Dept FG, 16 Chalk Hill, Watford, Herts WD1 4BN. Please add 50p per book as a contribution to postage and packing.